KZ & MK, Lord and Lady of the Lakes

A True Story of the Mystic Lakes Bald Eagles

By John Harrison & Kim Nagy

<u>Also by John Harrison and Kim Nagy</u>

Dead In Good Company:
A Celebration of Mount Auburn Cemetery

<u>True Wildlife Adventure Series for Children</u>

Skylar's Great Adventure
The True Story of a Brave Fresh Pond Owlet

Star Guy's Great Adventure
The True Story of a Salisbury Snowy Owl

Big Caesar's New Home
The True Story of a Coyote Season at Mount Auburn Cemetery

Wally & Wind of the Woburn Cliffs
The True Story of a Peregrine Falcon Family

Just ask the animals, and they will teach you.
Ask the birds of the sky, and they will tell you.
Speak to the earth, and it will instruct you.

JOB 12:7-8

Dedication

KZ & MK is dedicated to the next generation of Bald Eagle kids.

Oscar Kinsman, Sammy Kinsman, Simone Cruz, Quinn Hadley Paulson, Talya Feldman, Ilana Feldman, Henry Elias Maier, Ella Malvey, Benjamin French, Mason George Drudi, Jack Travis Drudi, Oaklyn Elizabeth Drudi, Layla Nathan, Tennessee Tuttle, Wallis Tuttle, Ella Higginson, Lucille Higginson, Madelyn Roussell, Patrick Roussell, Colin Roussell, Donovan Roussell, Bernadette Roussell, Sophia Matthews, Olivia Matthews, Violet Matthews, Ophelia Matthews, Saoirse Matthews, Canyon Tallman, Carrigan Tallman, Corby Scott Cunningham, Camry Cunningham, Cyler Cunningham, Abigail Parker, Oliver Woolverton Barnett, Olivia Wlodarczyk, Audrey Bradley, Addison Bradley, Amelia Bradley, Nel Rabens, Nora Rabens, Nathaniel Nearhood, Caitlin Gower, Nora Gower, Grace Gower, Katherine Rita Sullivan, Cheng-Loong, Cheng-Lin, Saddie Lesso, Adria Hadidian, Eliace Hadidian, Ellieah Marabella, Benjamin Marabella, Joshua Marabella, Francis Santarpio, Haidyn Santarpio, Willa Alford, Josie Alford, Harrison Balakier, Kenzie DeCoste, Olivia DiBari, Leo Gallagher, Lydia Harris, Ella Karp, Nola M., Everett O'Brien, Axcie Pucko, Lailah Rockwell, Arden Treadwell, Noah Welch, Layla Bryan, Ella Bryan, Carter Bryan, Jordan Brennan, John Connors, Thomas Anderson, Sophia Kimber, Ethan Leventhal, Riley Shay Doss, Maddie Lee Dahlbeck, Wyatt Dahlbeck, Grace Hanafin, Charlie Hanafin, Dylan Simard, Levi Simard, Celine Shedd, Remy Shedd, Elijah Shapiro,

Joshua Shapiro, Silvio Ortiz, Brayden Campbell, Jackson Campbell, Bennett Zalinski, Colin Zalinski, August Zalinski, Emma Manning, Jake Manning, Isabella Natalucci, Sophia Natalucci, Gio Natalucci, Declan Haley, Thomas Haley, Shay Shay, Nora Whalen, Brian Whalen, Henry Duval, John Duval, Zayah Asher Perlmutter, Caleb Jack Perlmutter, Mila Sage Perlmutter, Zachary Michael Kaplan, Cameron James Kaplan, Hannah Baron Silva, Ty Minogue, Kaelyn Minogue, Spencer Minogue, Nell Madigan Minogue, Eliana Minogue, Declan Minogue, Hazel Leslie, Lydia Leslie, Justin Williamson, Zinnia Lili Roehl-Gordon, Lamine Gordon, Madeline Rhunette Aandahl, Spencer David Aandahl, Bernadine DeMatteo, Annetta DeMatteo, Maggie Carey, Hugh Carey III, Annie Carey, Sofie Proulx, Sage Proulx, Sky Proulx, Shayne Proulx, Cannon Proulx, Patrick O'Neill, Emma O'Neill, Addison Hale, Isobel Hale, Brooks Camorali, Nathan Robert Gaskill, Pierce Edward Antonsen, Quinlan Grace Hagan, Shea Alice Hagan, Ryann Rose Hagan, Miles Hagan, Aurora Krueger, Ryanna Krueger, Parker Donahue, Jaxsen Daniel, Antonio Strate, Jack Sorrentino, Max Sorrentino, Mary Abigail McElwreath, Caroline Marguerite McElwreath, Evelyn Rose Riggs, Corinne Grace Riggs, Norah Lynn Riggs, Hailey Rene Riggs, Rhea Coogan, Della Coogan, Adrian Vogel, Sage Vogel, Oliver Vogel, Emma Vogel, Bailey Rose Sherman, Vivienne Sophia Sherman, Rose Charlotte Baker, Madeline DiGiorgio, Amelia DiGiorgio, Jocelyn Gesner, Ian Gesner, Evelyn Lamer, Owen Lamer, Ivan Lakits, Camille Horstman, Chesney Schlereth, Violet Nina, Noah Allen, Jude Allen and the grandchildren of the Boston Admirals Club employees.

One morning, just after sunrise, MK, a young Bald Eagle, left her nest along the shore and glided over the lake. Arlington was on her left, Medford was on her right, and Winchester was straight ahead.

She gracefully landed on 'The Tree,' a tall cottonwood behind the Medford Boat Club. 'The Tree' had been a usual perch place for Bald Eagles throughout the years, and it was given this distinction by local birdwatchers and photographers. 'The Tree' gave the eagles a 360-degree vista of the Mystic Lakes, which they needed, as fish is their primary diet.

Eagles need to know what's around them, because, in addition to fish, Bald Eagles will also eat ducks, squirrels and other mammals. Sometimes they will even steal food - especially from other eagles and fish-eating birds!

MK landed below KZ, her mate, who was already perched on a branch. On many mornings, at sunrise, watchers could witness the pair side by side on 'The Tree' with the morning sun shining on them like a spotlight.

How did the eagles get their names? MK and KZ were the letters on their leg bands, so that was what the people who watched called them.

Bands are sometimes affixed to young birds' legs before they fledge - their first flight - and the most important day in a young bird's life! A MassWildlife technician climbs to the nest, carefully collects the eaglets, and then takes them to the ground to be banded with an aluminum federal band and a larger, burnt-orange Massachusetts metal band with easier-to-read letters or numbers. These bands enable us to later identify the bird, including its age, sex and origin.

What did we know about MK? She was hatched in Waltham, Massachusetts in 2016. KZ's band told us that he had hatched in a Webster, MA nest in 2015.

Both MK and KZ were young adults. You could tell because there were still some brown smudges on their heads, especially on MK's forehead, the side of her head, and on her tail. Around the age of five, their brown heads and tails would likely turn pure white.

Bald Eagles, including young ones, have been at the Mystic Lakes for about two decades, mostly in the winter. Since 1998, up to fifteen migrant Bald Eagles a year have visited the Lakes. They come to the Lakes from their farther-north habitats because they need open water, especially during extreme cold spells, to fish and to catch other prey like ducks and coot.

In very cold winters, there were more Bald Eagle visitors. When spring arrived, the adult Bald Eagles would return to their northern homes. Until recently, no Bald Eagles would be seen at the lakes in summer.

MK and KZ began 'hanging out' in the fall of 2019. They were often seen together around the Lakes and especially on 'The Tree.'

In October, MK and KZ began to build a nest in an Arlington homeowner's backyard. This was the first Bald Eagle nest at the Mystic Lakes in at least a century!

Some considered MK and KZ to be too young to have a successful nest. It was possible, but unlikely. But MK and KZ didn't know that, so they continued working hard on their nest.

People who grew up around the Mystic Lakes never imagined that they would have a Bald Eagle nest - at the Lakes - one day! They thought Bald Eagle nests were in Alaska. Or maybe Maine. Or someplace else far away.

Today, there are more than 80 MassWildlife-documented Bald Eagle nests in Massachusetts. And thanks to the burnt-orange state bands, Massachusetts-hatched eagles have been confirmed breeding at nests in Connecticut and New York.

Bald Eagles, once a species in danger, are now thriving, thanks to the banning of the insecticide DDT in 1972. DDT and other pesticides have a catastrophic effect on wildlife and the environment. DDT thins the shells of the eagle (and other raptors') eggs, and they will likely break under the weight of the parent trying to incubate them.

As the years pass, we can expect to see more and more Bald Eagle nests in Massachusetts. The national symbol of our country is in good shape!

We learned a lot by watching MK and KZ. They were hard workers. We saw them land in trees or along the shore, break off branches with their talons, and then take them back to the nest they were building. They were constantly adding to their home.

What did their "home" look like? Bald Eagles are big birds and they have big nests - sometimes the nests are as large as ten feet wide and six feet deep!

In addition to branches the eagles acquired, they also would land on the ground and grasp a clump of grass, soft bark, or soft moss in their talons to bring back to the nest. This is the Bald Eagle version of wall-to-wall carpet. The grass or soft moss is where they lay their eggs. MK and KZ would fly from 'The Tree' to the grassy area around the Medford Boat Club to grab the moss and grass. We were lucky to be able to watch this activity!

Sometimes we could watch MK or KZ fish. They would fly above the Lakes looking down for movement. Have you ever heard the term 'eagle eye' to describe someone who has a keen ability to watch or observe? Eagles have excellent vision. They have sharper vision than we do, and their field of view is wider.

When they spotted a fish, the eagles would drop down and grab it off the surface in their talons. Then they would fly to a tree or return to their nest and eat the fish.

There were days when we wouldn't see the eagles at all. There were other nearby bodies of water where they could sometimes be found - Horn Pond in Woburn, Crystal Lake in Wakefield and Spy Pond in Arlington. They fly, so visiting nearby lakes and ponds is easy - and an adventure - for them. But mostly we could count on them being at the Lakes regularly during nesting season.

When we didn't see MK for a day, we wondered if maybe she had gone back to the nest in Waltham, where she was hatched, for a visit. MK's dad remained in Waltham and has had at least three different mates over the past several years.

Since MK was hatched in Waltham, her dad has been the father of at least four eaglets. So, MK has half-brothers and sisters. Because these eaglets were banded by MassWildlife before they fledged, we might learn about their future travels.

MK's Waltham relatives were also exciting to watch! Their habitat, being a cemetery, was very open. In the spring, we would see MK's dad fly from the nest and head toward trees in the distance. He would return carrying a branch and then he would position it in the nest. His mate also brought in branches. Sometimes they would fight about the positioning of the branches in the nest. And we could watch these little disagreements!

This Waltham family occasionally landed on the grass and on memorials! They would perch on trees in the cemetery, often right above us. We had plenty of opportunities to watch them. Sometimes the young eaglets would fly together and then perch next to each other.

After eaglets are hatched, they spend a few months being fed by mom and dad, and learning to hunt. Then, in the fall, they leave their parents. The young eaglets strike out on their own — searching for good hunting locations and socializing with other, especially young, eagles. They will likely not begin looking for territory or a mate until they are 4 or 5 years old.

In the fall, when the young eaglets are on their own, the adult eagles will begin to refurbish the nest for their next family. Usually, a pair of eagles will re-use the same nest, also called an aerie. Bald Eagle nests have to be big enough to accommodate up to five Bald Eagles - mom and dad and up to three eaglets. This requires a lot of work from the eagle couple each year because the rough winters in the north degrade the nests over the season.

One day, in mid-April, a scary thing happened. An adult male Bald Eagle, Z74 on his band, became interested in MK and KZ's nest. This sometimes happens with eagles. Lone eagles will attempt to intrude into an active nest. Usually, it's a male Bald Eagle that does this, but sometimes females disrupt an active nest too. This eagle, from Western New York, wanted to take over the nest and drive KZ away. Watchers named this eagle 'New York' since he was hatched there.

New York - Z74

New York made many attempts to disrupt the nest. Once KZ was seen in the air rolling over in flight and lifting his talons in defense from Z74.They locked talons and spiraled head-over-heels, plummeting until no longer visible. This worried the usual bunch of watchers at the dam. For adult Bald Eagles, locking talons means intense fighting.

New York - Z74

This aggressive behavior continued for more than a month before it stopped. KZ was observed driving away at least six adult male interlopers that season. Bald Eagles - and all birds, really - have to always be prepared for disruption and aggression even from their own species. In fact, *especially* from other Bald Eagles!

New York - Z74

We knew that MK and KZ's first nest attempt only had a 50-50 chance of succeeding, because they were young and inexperienced. Their first attempt did fail, but they had learned how to build a nest, defend territory, and work together. From this experience, including chasing off adult intruders, the bond between MK and KZ grew even stronger.

Next year, they will be older and better prepared to have a family. And they already have a nest for their second attempt. We hoped that in the fall and winter we would see MK and KZ flying to their nest with branches - a signal that they were trying again. We were all looking forward to this, and we hoped that the next year would bring little eaglets hatched at the Mystic Lakes for the first time in recent history, where they would eventually fly like the eagles they were, high above us, wild and free!

MassWildlife and Bald Eagles

MassWildlife and Bald Eagles

MassWildlife, headquartered in the town of Westborough, MA, has many responsibilities. The organization's mission is the conservation of freshwater fish and wildlife in Massachusetts and, additionally, MassWildlife's Natural Heritage & Endangered Species Program is responsible for protecting the Commonwealth's wide range of rare biological diversity. It endeavors to restore, protect and manage land for wildlife to thrive and for people to enjoy. MassWildlife is the principal caretaker of Bald Eagles in Massachusetts.

Bald Eaglet Banding, May 21, 2019

David Paulson, Senior Endangered Species Review Biologist for the Massachusetts Division of Fisheries & Wildlife, Natural Heritage and Endangered Species Program, noted that as of 2020 there were at least 80 active eagle nests throughout Massachusetts. Especially exciting is that in Barnstable in 2020, there was an eagle nest that fledged a chick (banded with 73/B color band) - the first time on Cape Cod in 115 years. The last active eagle's nest was in Sandwich in 1905. The Bald Eagle, our national symbol, is thriving and the population is growing in the Bay State.

Dave Paulson, Senior Endangered Species Review Biologist
for the Massachusetts Division of Fisheries & Wildlife,
Natural Heritage and Endangered Species Program

Many of the active nests have been monitored for decades. Andrew Vitz, Mass State Ornithologist, organizes these efforts with the MassWildlife District staff and volunteers. There is an ongoing effort to monitor as many nests as possible but factors such as accessibility, familiarity with the site and geographic significance of the nest all play a part in the prioritization.

Dr. Andrew Vitz, Mass State Ornithologist,
banding an American Kestrel

Banding of the eaglet hatchlings is another priority. The number of nests that are annually banded depends on several factors - staff availability (banding requires qualified climbers), the integrity of the nest tree (is it safe), and site accessibility. MassWildlife bands other species too (Peregrine Falcons, American Kestrels, song birds, terns, Canada Geese and American Black Duck), which is another important part of the mission

MassWildlife Peregrine Falcon
Banding, June 15, 2020

How many Bald Eagle nests produce hatchlings? At the end of the 2018 monitoring season, 36 nests produced 63 eagle chicks. Of these 63 chicks, 42 were banded with a USGS federal band and a field readable color band identifying each individual.

2019: 72 active nests, 68 fledglings, 32 chicks banded

2020: 80 active nests, and only 2 chicks banded (due to restrictions from pandemic)

Bald Eagle Active Pairs 1987-2020

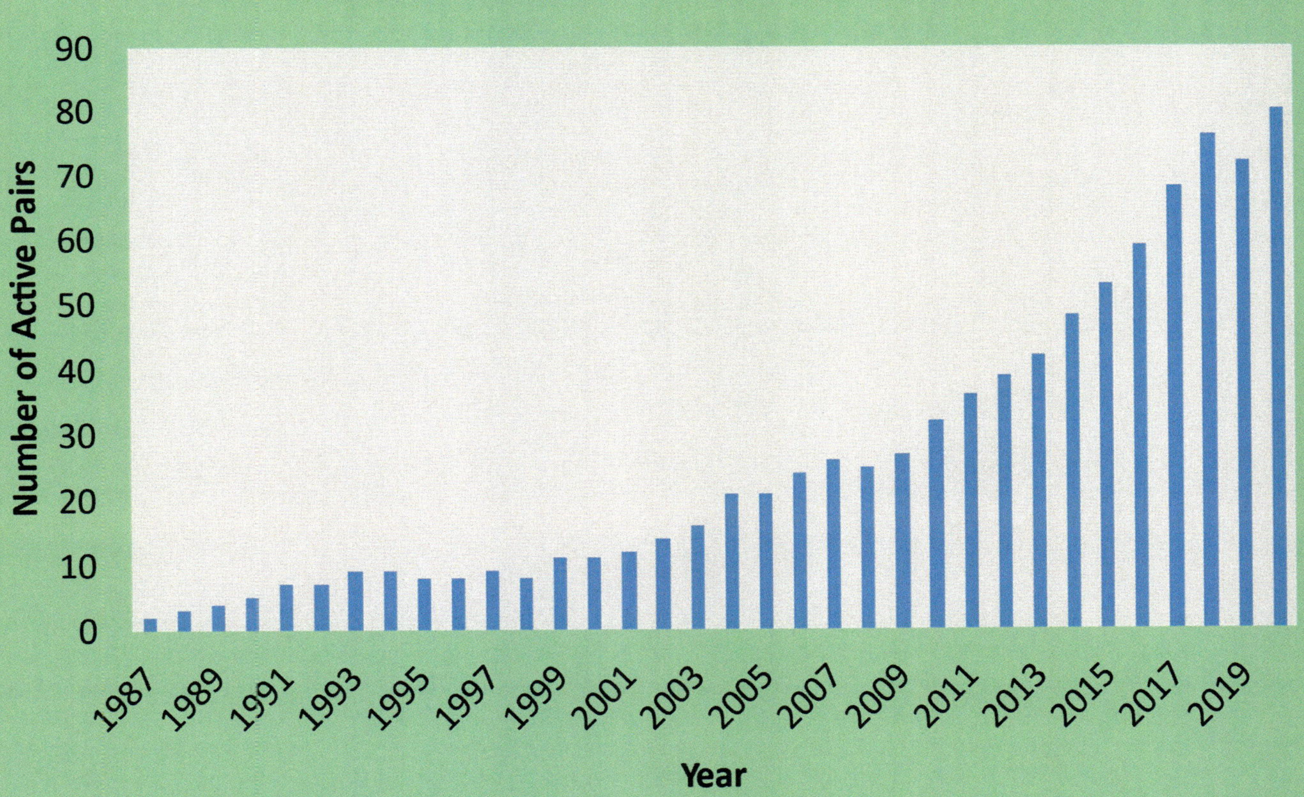

2020 marked the 32nd year since their restoration that Bald Eagles have raised young in Massachusetts. Since 1989, the number of known territorial pairs of Bald Eagles in MA has increased to 80. During these 32 years, at least 873 wild-born chicks are known to have fledged, and an additional 8 chicks that were captive-born and fostered have also fledged (881 chicks in total). MassWildlife's efforts are keeping our Bald Eagle population healthy. Hopefully, as the years go by, there will be many more first-time nests for people to enjoy like the one on the Mystic Lakes.

For further information about MassWildlife, visit their website:
www.mass.gov/orgs/division-of-fisheries-and-wildlife

For further information about other Conservation Success Stories:
www.mass.gov/service-details/rare-species-success-stories

Ways to Support Endangered Species Conservation:
www.mass.gov/service-details/support-endangered-species-conservation

The Natural Heritage & Endangered Species Program is responsible for the conservation and protection of hundreds of species that are not hunted, fished, trapped, or commercially harvested in the state, as well as the protection of the natural communities that make up their habitats.

BALD EAGLE FACTS

- The Bald Eagle is the only eagle native to North America. Their normal range includes northern Mexico, all of the continental United States, and most of Canada.

- There have been confirmed Massachusetts nests at Quabbin Reservoir, along the Connecticut and Merrimack Rivers, and on lakes in Plymouth County. The first confirmed nest at a Mass Audubon wildlife sanctuary was at Arcadia Wildlife Sanctuary in 2012.

- The largest Bald Eagle nest of record is near St. Petersburg, Florida. It also is listed in the Guinness Book of World Records. It was measured in 1963, and was found to be 9.5 feet wide and 20 feet deep. It was estimated to weigh 4,409 pounds.

- Bald Eagles usually nest in trees. They prefer to be as high as possible and near a body of water. The Bald Eagle measures from 28 to 40 inches and their wing span is six to seven feet. Females are about 30% larger than males. Size and weight depends on their geographic location.

- The eagle's eyes are among the strongest of any animal. They are estimated to be four to eight times stronger than human eyes.

- The greatest threat to wildlife is habitat loss, as well as invasive species, and pesticides/environmental chemicals. Bald Eagles face additional threats from an increased human population, logging, and the development of waterfront property.

- Baby chicks are fully grown in nine weeks. Once their wing and tail feathers have developed, the fledgling can leave the nest. Sometimes the parents will encourage the fledglings to fly by forcing them out of the nest.

- It takes up to five years for eagles to reach adulthood. Then the eagle will begin to look for a mate and establish a territory. The territory is usually located withing 250 miles of where they were originally hatched. Eagles have a lifespan of 30 to 35 years in the wild, and up to 50 years in captivity.

- The Bald Eagle is our National Symbol. The eagle's association with authority stems back to Roman times. Our Founding Fathers liked the idea of an eagle because it also symbolized strength, freedom, courage and power. The hope was that these qualities mirrored those of the newly formed nation of America.

- Conowingo Dam, a Hydro Station in Maryland, is an excellent place to see eagles catch fish in the early winter months. Magee Marsh Wildlife Area in Ottawa County, Ohio, on the shores of Lake Erie, is another good place to view eagles.

- You can help the birds, yourself and the environment by eating fruits and vegetables that have not been sprayed by pesticides and other chemicals.

Conowingo Dam

Magee Marsh

ACKNOWLEDGMENTS

We give special thanks to our first readers: Bobbie Gatz, Dr. Mariana Castells, Sharon Sherman, Corinne Kinsman, Laura and Steve Duggan, Don and Geri Tremblay, Ursula and Dave Goodine, and Cyn McCarthy.

Our gratitude for: Corinne and Artty Kinsman, Peter Filichia, Linda Konner, Upton Bell, JoAnne O'Neill, Paul Treseler, Ray Cilley, Lloyd Torgove, Bob and Edie Di Giorgio, James Harrison, Mary Hogan, Joe Plati, Joe and Karen Polvere, Keith and Cathy Joyce, Bob and Becky Parsons, Mark Nickerson, Chaz and Virginia Brown, Nell Coakley, Ray Brown of Talkin' Birds, Gary Goshgarian, William Martin, Cathy and Dick Minogue, Frank and Bobbie Gatz, John Amaral, Sangeet Kaur Khalsa, Hank Philippi Ryan, Sandy and Don Selesky, Jim and Patty Sears-Joyce, Sharon Kennedy, Dawna Blum of Wild Birds Unlimited, our Wildlife Whisperer John Sullivan and - always - Steve Gladstone, who brings ideas and manuscripts to life.

Special thanks to Paul Roberts, Medford's Raptor Scholar, for his insights into the Bald Eagle species.

Special thanks to Dave Paulson, Senior Endangered Species Review Biologist for the Massachusetts Division of Fisheries & Wildlife, Natural Heritage and Endangered Species Program and Dr. Andrew Vitz, Mass State Ornitholigist, for their efforts to make KZ and MK soar!

Thank you Michael Armanious, Jeff Munro, Katie Chang, Jonathan Barbato, Norm McLeod and the staff of Arlington Community Media for your continuing support and for making our Dead In Good Company video, Skylar's Great Adventure videos and the Conversations With Great Authors video series.

And lastly, in loving memory of our friends in wildlife - Ernie Sarro, Virginia Parsons and Deb Cilley.

PHOTO CREDITS

- John Harrison: front cover and pages 3, 7, 15, 17, 21, 23, 29, 31, 37, 43, 45, 47, 49, 51, 57, 71, 77, 83, 95.
- Kim Nagy: back cover and pages 33, 41, 53, 55, 59, 61, 63, 73, 91.
- Patty Sears-Joyce: page 9
- Judd Nathan: page 11
- Paul Roberts: page 13
- David Morris: page 19
- Jim Renault: page 25
- Ken Stampfer: page 27
- Nancy Gower: page 35
- Steve Giurlando: page 39
- John Blout: page 65
- Stephen Bottari: page 67
- Jason Bottari: page 69
- Troy Gipps: pages 74, 79, 81
- Paul Treseler: page 90
- Photo conversion to illustration by Steve Gladstone

ABOUT THE AUTHORS

John Harrison and Kim Nagy are the Editors of *Dead in Good Company*, a compelling collection of essays, poems and wildlife photographs of Mount Auburn Cemetery in Cambridge, Massachusetts. Sweet Auburn, as it's affectionately known, is America's first garden cemetery, and *Dead in Good Company* is the first book to celebrate the Cemetery as a place of regeneration and transformation; the circle of life. Mount Auburn Cemetery is one of New England's Birding Hotspots.

Skylar's Great Adventure: The True Story of a Brave Fresh Pond Owlet, Star Guy's Great Adventure: The True Story of a Salisbury Snowy Owl, Big Caesar's New Home: The True Story of a Coyote Season at Mount Auburn Cemetery and **Wally & Wind of the Woburn Cliffs:** *The True Story of a Peregrine Falcon Family* are the first books in the True Wildlife Adventure series. See more at: www.facebook.com/deadingoodcompany and on YouTube: https://www.youtube.com/watch?v=cFwi69Uk2-4&feature=youtu.be&app=desktop

John Harrison Founded Epilog Enterprises, a book distribution company, in 1975. His passion for nature ultimately led to the idea for this book. His photographs have been published by Mass Audubon, the Humane Society of the United States, and Project Coyote in CA, and have appeared in books, calendars, magazines, newspapers, and websites. He lectures on nature and wildlife at elementary schools and to senior citizen groups. Additionally, he authored the *Medford Wildlife Watch* blog for The Medford Transcript newspaper for ten years.

Kim Nagy has made the natural world both her profession and her hobby. She is an avid wildlife and nature photographer, and travels widely in pursuit of her craft. She works as a National Sales Manager in the natural products industry. Her photos have appeared in National Geographic's Daily Dozen, *BirdWatching, The BirdNote* calendar, several publications of the Massachusetts Audubon Society, *The Marco Review, Tin Mountain Conservation Center* and more (photo by Ray Cilley).

See more at: www.facebook.com/catchlightphotos

Lord and Lady of the Lakes

Made in the USA
Monee, IL
21 March 2021

62556047R00059